Making Garden Meadows

How to create a natural haven for wildlife

Jenny Steel

Brambleby Books

Making Garden Meadows – How to create a natural haven for wildlife
Copyright © Jenny Steel 2013

Jenny Steel has asserted her right under the Copyright,
Design and Patent Act, 1988, to be identified as author of this work.

A CIP catalogue record for this book is available from the British Library

ISBN 9781908241221

Published 2013 by
Brambleby Books Ltd., UK
www.bramblebybooks.co.uk

Cover design and layout by Creatix Design
Cover photo by Jenny Steel

Printed and bound by Cambrian Printers, UK
FSC and PFSC accredited

Making
Garden
Meadows

Small Tortoiseshell on Common Knapweed

About the Author

Jenny Steel developed a passion for wildlife when she discovered caterpillars at the age of six and an interest in birds and wildflowers soon followed. Her mother's enthusiasm for gardening and her father's part-time occupation in journalism and photography were also instrumental in her career path.

A degree in Applied Biology was followed by a Master's Degree in Plant Ecology based on her research into woodland ecosystems in Wytham Woods, Oxford University's well-studied 'outdoor laboratory'. More work in the University's Department of Plant Sciences followed and concluded with a six-year project studying arable weeds.

In 1990 she left the University to set up a wildflower nursery, providing native plants and insect-attracting cottage garden plants for wildlife gardeners. Her writing career began with regular pieces in the award-winning *Limited Edition Magazine*, a sister publication to *the Oxford Times*, and she became a regular contributor to BBC Radio Oxford. More writing work followed for a variety of publications, including *Organic Gardening Magazine*, *The Countryman*, *Spaces Magazine*, *BBC Gardens Illustrated* and *BBC Easy Gardening*. She appeared on the BBC gardening programmes *Gardener's World* and as a presenter on *How Does Your Garden Grow*.

In 2005, she moved from her native Oxfordshire to South Shropshire where she and her husband have created a two-acre wildlife garden. She is a keen photographer, and her writing and images are inspired by the wildlife and countryside around her and further afield.

Preface

I grew up in Oxford where my mother tended – with great passion and skill – a tiny garden at the back of a Victorian terrace. This garden at various times housed chickens and bantams, a pond full of Great Crested Newts, borders of prize-winning Dahlias and bumblebee nests. Swifts and House Sparrows nested under the eaves and Robins in the rose arch. These early years established my interest in wildlife as an integral part of a garden, although at that time the term wildlife gardening hadn't been invented.

In spite of living in the middle of a small city, my parents were both country folk, and as a family our focus was on the local countryside or the stately river that runs through Oxford's centre. It was a short walk from my home to the water meadows alongside the Thames at Iffley, in spring a swathe of Lady's Smock and Ragged Robin. As a family we made a yearly pilgrimage to Otmoor or Ducklington to see fritillary meadows full of the chequered bells of this beautiful plant together with, in my memory at least, acres of Cowslips. The Bluebell woods of the Chilterns were also a regular haunt. I grew up with all this around me but didn't at the time realise how much these walks and visits would influence my career path.

Once I had a home and garden of my own I began to appreciate how important my early gardening and wildlife experiences had been. Much as I loved the plants I was growing, my real

Green-veined White on Greater Knapweed

Oxeye Daisies

interest was in the wildlife that visited these plants, and encouraging birds, mammals and invertebrates into my successively larger and larger gardens became the objective, even though this was seen as being rather odd! And as these ideas progressed, the concept of a garden meadow, something like a tiny version of the wonderful wild meadows I knew, began to present itself as an attainable goal.

In recent times the creation of garden meadows, both large and small, has become fashionable. At Highgrove the enlightened gardener HRH the Prince of Wales has planted meadows full of wildflowers and non-natives to great effect, which has helped to popularise this way of gardening. Whilst acres may be desirable, this book is intended to help you make a small garden meadow of your own using native flowers and grasses.

Meadows encourage a range of invertebrates, birds and mammals that you might otherwise not see in your garden and could greatly increase the biodiversity of your local area. They provide a breeding area for butterflies, seeds for birds, and food and shelter for amphibians and small mammals. A meadow will also give you the opportunity to grow a range of native wildflowers in a stunning setting. In short, a wildflower meadow is one of the most exciting habitats you can add to your garden, and I hope this book will both inspire and help you to create your own.

Jenny Steel, May 2013

9

Contents

CHAPTER FIVE

CHAPTER SIX

CHAPTER SEVEN

APPENDIX

Meadow early summer

Meadow mid-summer

CHAPTER ONE

An Introduction to Wildflower Meadows and Cornfield Flower Areas

Over the past twenty years gardening has changed and evolved into something quite different from the activity carried out by our parents and grandparents. For many of them gardening was mainly about growing food as we emerged from the troubled times of the 1930s and 1940s when borders were more likely to contain sprouts and cauliflowers than evergreen shrubs or wildflowers. But many things have transformed our countryside over the last 50 years. Climate change, the introduction of new farm crops such as rape and plants for biofuels plus the degradation of wildlife habitats has meant that many more gardeners want to manage their own little piece of land in a very different way to how our parents did in the past. Growing wildflowers has become commonplace, 45 per cent of all households feed the birds in some way, and most of us are much more conscious of the wildlife that uses our gardens. The changes that have come about in gardening have been beneficial to us as garden users and especially to the creatures that visit or make their homes in our gardens.

More and more gardeners want to recreate a little bit of countryside in their own plot where wildlife can find a safe home and creating an area of wild grasses and flowers in the garden – a proper wildflower meadow – is often a top priority. We see this wonderful kind of habitat in television programmes or even in advertisements, in dreamy photos of sunlit daisies and tawny grasses in magazines or simply remember visiting fabulous hayfields in our youth. For me, it was definitely memories of those visits which prompted me to start creating wildflower meadows in my gardens, along with the knowledge that meadows are brilliant for wildlife.

Meadow grasses

Snake's Head Fritillary

Oxeye Daisy with hoverfly

Wildflower meadow

Meadow Cranesbill

Common Knapweed

I was brought up in Oxford where the River Thames meanders through water meadows full of Snake's Head Fritillaries and Lady's Smock in spring, and Yellow Rattle, Moon or Oxeye Daisies and Knapweed in summer. These places always seemed to have clouds of butterflies rising above them, birds in the hedges all around, whilst the air was full of the sounds of buzzing insects. They were idyllic places, and I wanted one of my own! For many of us wildflower meadows are evocative of the past, reminding us of the countryside, even if we live in a city, and look wild and beautiful throughout the spring, summer and autumn. But most importantly for the wildlife gardener, or anyone with an interest in gardening *with* nature, rather than against it, a meadow really does attract, nurture and provide shelter for species of insect, mammal and bird unlikely to be found anywhere else in a garden.

What is a meadow?

Before we look at creating this habitat in our garden, it is important to understand just what we mean by the word 'meadow'. A meadow in the countryside can be many different things, and each wild meadow is unique in its composition of plants and animals. Most people who are interested in creating an area of grass and flowers in their garden or want to convert an area of lawn to an approximation of that wild habitat will have in their minds an image of the traditional hay meadow brimming over with many species of wild flower, including

Cranesbill, Knapweed, Oxeye Daisy and Lady's Bedstraw. Dainty grass heads weave their way through the flowers, and butterflies, bumblebees and other insects dance over the grasses and flowers in the sunshine, and grasshoppers chirp from the depths. The good news is that this rural idyll is achievable, up to a point. Strictly speaking though, we are referring to creating a 'meadow effect'. The traditional hay meadow just described would have taken hundreds of years of time-honoured management to create, including winter grazing by animals plus cutting and baling the hay, in order to achieve a colourful and unique tapestry of plants and their attendant wildlife. In a garden though, you can recreate an approximation of this habitat, and some of the spectacular wildlife that depends

Oxeye Daisy

upon these plants will undoubtedly visit your garden if you do.

So throughout this guide the word 'meadow' will be used to describe any area of wild grasses and flowers, whether that be the summer hay meadow of your imagination or a spring meadow with Lady's Smock

Lady's Bedstraw

Lady's Smock

Meadow grasses

and Cowslips. However, it is important to understand that a meadow is composed largely of grasses – as much as 80 per cent – and these are crucial to the habitat as a whole and the wildlife that uses it.

What about poppies?

When talking to people about creating meadow areas in gardens I often hear the words, 'I really want a meadow full of poppies'! This technically would not be a meadow, as poppies only grow for a very limited time amongst grasses – they are annual wildflowers, and meadows are largely composed of perennial grasses and flowers. But this book is about creating both **garden meadows** and what are often known as **'cornfield flower areas'**, and there is plenty of confusion about what those terms mean. A meadow does not generally contain poppies, Cornflowers, Corncockle or other

Corn Poppies

annual wildflowers, at least not for long. These colourful annuals, which so many people love, used to grow in profusion on the edges of arable fields in the countryside and need freshly disturbed open soil, such as they would find after ploughing or sowing, in order to spread and flourish. They are transient and temporary (although we can manipulate our gardens to ensure they seed from year to year). So if you imagine your grassy meadow filled with red poppies, forget that dream. If you include poppies with your grass, they will persist for a couple of years only and then die out as they will soon run out of bare areas in which to germinate. But these lovely annuals can be grown very successfully in even small gardens. A special cornfield flower area addresses that problem by creating beds specifically for these luscious, colourful annuals. The grass is left out which means that the annuals are not competing for space with other dense

vegetation. A cornfield flower area is brilliant for wildlife, as the individual species provide lots of nectar and pollen for bees, butterflies, hoverflies and pollen beetles amongst other invertebrates. If you want a bright area of colourful wildflowers, these annuals can be grown with ease, and they are suitable for a space of any size, as long as it is in full sun. Chapter 6 has details about making an area of cornfield annuals, together with information about some of the wildlife that an area like this will attract.

To summarise, **garden meadows are permanent features that remain largely undisturbed through the spring and summer months and contain mainly perennial plants – grasses plus wildflowers that will grow and spread from year to year. Cornfield flower areas are annual flowers alone, with no perennial grasses.**

The wildlife in your garden meadow

Hay meadows in our countryside are very special in many ways, but in particular they have a great variety of wildlife associated with them. Because of the shelter meadows provide to small creatures, it is likely that even a tiny meadow area in a garden could be a place where lots of wildlife will find a home. Our native wildflowers and grasses will, in any situation, always have a whole host of small invertebrates feeding upon them. This mass of creatures attracts specific insect-eating

Robin

Wren

Fox

birds such as Robins, Wrens and tits all year round, but at breeding time virtually all birds will be searching for these insects for their fledglings. Lots of smaller mammals, including shrews, Field Mice, voles and Hedgehogs, will also feed on these creatures. The smaller mammals in their turn may encourage larger mammals such as Foxes and Weasels to the garden or even predatory birds, especially Kestrels, as these feed largely on voles and mice. Reptiles and amphibians can also find food and shelter in a meadow. The seeds of the grasses and wildflowers will attract the seed-eating bird species, especially the finches – Goldfinches, Linnets, Greenfinches, Chaffinches and Bullfinches. Over time, a whole web of inter-dependent life will be created around your meadow habitat, and a food chain will evolve whereby each creature is dependant upon a plant, or another creature, for food. Plus all will appreciate the undisturbed nature of the habitat.

Kestrel

Common Frog

Chaffinch, a seed-eater

It is well known that meadows are especially good for butterflies. In particular there are several that lay their eggs on native grasses, although they are fairly specific about the types of grass they need. Meadow Brown, Ringlet, Gatekeeper, Marbled White and the lovely little skipper butterflies are a few of the species that use some of our native grasses as their larval food plants – that is the plants that their caterpillars feed on. This means that long grass in a meadow may encourage these butterflies, not just to visit your garden but to breed there too. So creating a wildflower meadow is an important way to help these insects.

Butterflies clockwise from top left: **Ringlet, Meadow Brown, Small Skipper, Gatekeeper**

19

Meadow during mid-summer

Cornfield Flower Area

A **garden meadow's** strength lies in two things – its range and mix of species of plants and animals, and the fact that it is undisturbed for long periods which means that wildlife has a chance to get established. The long grasses and wildflowers come to provide homes for too many creatures to mention, all existing in a habitat that, over time, nature (i.e. selection, ecological adaptation and evolution) has forged to take account of their needs and life cycles.

A **cornfield flower area** with annual wildflowers will attract a different range of wildlife. Like a wildflower meadow, it remains undisturbed for most of the summer and will therefore provide a sheltered home for small mammals and lots of ground-dwelling and plant-eating insects. The mix of wildflowers generally includes Corn Poppy, Cornflower, Corn Marigold, Corncockle and Corn Chamomile, and these provide plenty of pollen

Clockwise from top left: **Common Blue, Corn Marigold with hoverfly, Cornflower with bumblebee, Goldfinch**

and nectar for insects. The nectar in the Cornflowers attracts smaller species of butterfly, such as the Common Blue, and the poppies are a fantastic hoverfly attractant because they have masses of pollen for the adult flies to feed on. Corn Marigolds will have a whole host of small bees and bumblebees visiting them for their nectar and pollen. A cornfield flower area provides a blaze of colour which buzzes with insect life. Later in the autumn when the summer flowers go over, Goldfinches find the seeds of the Cornflowers irresistible.

Non-native flowers in a meadow

So far we have assumed that garden meadows should have a range of native wildflowers growing with the wild grasses. Undoubtedly a habitat such as this will be best for your local wildlife, but it is possible to include non-native flowers and bulbs in a meadow area to enhance the way it looks and possibly its wildlife-attracting power. This is fine if you wish to try it, but it is probable that **the more native plants you include the wider the range of wildlife you will attract.** However, if you do wish to create a meadow area with some non-native flowers, you will need to put a little extra work into your choice of plants. Only certain types of perennial plants will survive for any length of time in grass, so you will need to try to choose plants that you know have good pollen and nectar-producing properties as

Echinacea and Peacock Butterfly

well as the ability to grow in a grassy sward. Flowers such as *Echinacea* and *Rudbeckia* grow in meadow or 'prairie' conditions in the US and can be encouraged to establish in a meadow here.

Before you get started

The descriptions above and the photographs in this little book may have kindled your enthusiasm, but one thing to consider at this stage is the amount of work involved. Meadows and wildflower areas do not look after themselves. Although they can be a way of reducing work in the garden, there is still quite a lot of maintenance associated with them. Chapter 7 will give you an idea of the maintenance involved.

Pyramidal Orchid

Before you go any further, take a good look at your garden to **see what already exists** there. If you have just moved to a new plot, try leaving small areas of lawn unmown for one summer to see what comes up. Occasionally gardens of older houses (or paddocks and orchards) already have a good supply of interesting wildflowers, particularly if the grasses are fine-leaved native species. Many wildflowers can survive unseen for years in areas that are mown or grazed only to pop up and flower when they are given the opportunity. I have even heard of gardens where large areas of orchids have appeared once this cautious approach was taken. Only remove turf and re-sow with meadow seed when you are absolutely sure that there is nothing of interest or beauty living there already.

Once you are certain that you want to pursue your dream of a garden meadow or a wildflower area, the other chapters in this book will help you to decide where to put it, how to prepare the site, sow seed or add plants, and how to look after the area once it is established.

Yorkshire Fog

CHAPTER TWO
Making a Meadow from Seed

So far we have looked at how special designated areas within a garden can be helped to become suitable habitats for a variety of wildlife, and for many of us this is the most important reason for developing an area such as this in our gardens. However, gardens are vital extensions of our homes, and thus we want to ensure that, if we are to include an area of wildflowers such as this, it enhances our enjoyment of the garden and the way it looks. All too often garden meadows revert to long grass and little else, much to the disappointment of the gardener.

This important chapter outlines the steps you will need to take to ensure that you establish your meadow successfully. It assumes that you are starting with an area of bare soil where existing plants, including grasses, have been removed. Chapter 7 is equally important as it describes the work you will need to do to ensure that your meadow looks the way you want it to be for years to come. The establishment of a cornfield flower area is described in Chapter 6.

Choosing your site

In a small garden there may be little room for choice when it comes to deciding where your meadow area will be. However, one thing is quite important. Most seed mixtures for establishing meadows – 'meadow mixes' – will contain species that prefer to grow

Native grasses

in full sun. Specialist growers of native seed will also have mixtures suitable for light shade or for woodland situations; so if your area is even slightly shaded, consider one of these alternatives or try a spring meadow as outlined in Chapter 4. Sowing and maintenance of the area will be more or less the same whether it is in sun or shade, but make sure that you choose the appropriate mixture of plants for your conditions.

Type of soil

If you are fortunate enough to have an open sunny spot, you will next need to decide what type of soil you have. Wildflowers establish more easily in soil of low fertility, so it is unwise to choose a spot that has been fertilised over many years. In richer soils the grasses may grow more quickly than the wildflowers, which can result in the flowers being swamped. If you have a fertile soil, you will need to take action before sowing.

Dealing with fertile soil

It may be necessary to deal with the problem of fertile soil even before you decide on the type of meadow you would like in the garden. This can be done in a variety of ways, but none of them is particularly easy!

- The first option is to plant and harvest a 'hungry' crop such as potatoes. This ties up the area for a whole season, or even two, thus delaying your plans. Not an option for the impatient, but it can work effectively. The potatoes will use up nitrogen in the soil, reducing its fertility for the benefit of the wildflowers to come.

- The second option is to remove some of your fertile soil and replace it with something less wholesome. If you are creating a wildlife pond in the garden, the soil from the very bottom of the hole will be ideal. Replace 15 or 20 cm (6 or 8 inches) of your top soil throughout the proposed meadow area with this low fertility soil, and your meadow should establish with no problems. Subsoil can also be purchased and imported into the garden if necessary.

- The third option is more interesting and involves a plant called Yellow Rattle, and there is more information about this plant in Chapter 3.

- If all this sounds like too much work, try sowing a cornfield flower patch instead (see Chapter 6). The annual

Cornfield flower patch

wildflowers in a mixture such as this are more tolerant of greater fertility and, as no grass is present in the seed mix, there is no chance of the flowers being swamped by the more aggressive grasses. Your area will be different in nature and will attract a different range of animals, birds and insects, but it will still enhance the garden visually and make it more wildlife friendly. Plus it is possible to convert an area such as this to a proper grassy meadow when the fertility has dropped.

When you are happy with the fertility of the soil you can think about the meadow mix seed you will need.

As gardeners, we all know that some plants will grow for us and others won't. This is dependant on a few factors, one of which – the amount of light in the garden – we have mentioned above. The second factor is the type of soil you have. **First find out about the**

Meadow seed mix

type of soil you have. Your soil may be free draining, sandy or clay that dries out in the summer but is waterlogged in winter, acid, alkaline, or several combinations of these. Wildflowers, contrary to what many of us believe, can be very fussy about the conditions in which they grow well. One thing is certain – there is absolutely no point in attempting to grow plants that are not suited to your soil. You will be wasting money, seed and time, and be disappointed into the bargain. It is therefore vital that you find out a little about your soil and choose a meadow mix that is suitable for your conditions.

It will probably be fairly obvious if your soil is free draining and light – you will be able to grow plants like lavender and rosemary, which prefer the easy drainage, without them dying off in the winter. You may find that you can leave dahlias in the soil over the winter, and they survive until the spring. In a heavy clay soil they would succumb to

the cold and damp conditions and not survive. If you have a clay soil, it will be difficult to work in the winter, be heavy and waterlogged after rain and hold together in lumps. A pH-testing kit from your local garden centre will indicate whether you have acid or alkaline soil. Hopefully it will not be too difficult a task to ascertain roughly what type of soil you are dealing with. If you can't, use a 'general purpose' meadow mix which will contain species of wild flower that aren't too fussy about the conditions they can adapt to. A meadow of this type will still have a good variety of flowers and be a great habitat for wildlife.

Deciding on your meadow seed

Once you have determined your soil type the specialist seed growers have made all the difficult decisions for you. They will be able to supply you with a mixture of grasses and wildflowers perfectly adapted to your particular soil type. Alternatively, simply go for a general-purpose mix, which will have unfussy wildflowers that can cope with a range of soil types. What is really important about these seed mixtures is that, if they are bought from a reputable grower (see the information on page 63), they will only contain seed of native origin. This means that the species contained there will all be plants that our native wildlife is used to and adapted to feeding on. Seed imported from other countries, even if the species names are the same as our wild plants, can still have subtle differences as far as wildlife is concerned and should be avoided. Most mixtures will contain six or seven different wild grasses and a selection of native wildflowers that will grow happily with the grasses. These mixtures will also not have 'agricultural' varieties of our wildflowers. These have been bred to produce bigger, often leafier plants suitable for animal grazing and can swamp our own more delicate wildflowers.

Preparing the ground for sowing

Since this chapter is about creating a new meadow from seed, the approach will only work really well if you have an area of bare soil in front of you. Before you go any further, **the ground must be cleared of perennial weeds** which will persist indefinitely if you

don't get rid of them at the very start of your project. Some annuals are likely to pop up whether you want them or not, but these will soon disappear with the correct maintenance over time. If you garden organically, dig out nettles, thistles, docks and Couch Grass by hand, or you could cover them with black polythene, newspaper or even old carpet. Covering weeds of this type will only work if all light is excluded for several months; so again, plan ahead if your potential meadow area has weed cover of this sort. If you are converting an area of lawn, the turf must be removed. This can be a laborious process by hand, but it is now possible to rent turf cutters from tool-hire companies. When using one of these machines, make sure you take all

Nettle

Spear Thistle

Ready to sow

the safety precautions recommended. Turf can be re-used elsewhere in the garden or stacked up in an out-of-the-way place where it will break down over time to produce useful potting compost.

When the soil is cleared it will need to be turned over with a fork and raked down to a fine tilth. On larger areas a rotovator can be used, but bear in mind that the more the soil is turned over the greater the number of weed seeds will be turned up. These could include docks, thistles, various grasses, Fat-hen and Groundsel all common weeds in our gardens. These must then be dealt with, especially the perennials, by hoeing or digging out. Inevitably there will be weeds left behind, but the more you can remove from the soil at this stage, the more successful your meadow will be.

Sowing your meadow mix

Meadows can be sown at almost any time, but for the beginner **spring (March or April) or autumn (September or October) are the easiest times to get started.** A spring sowing is preferred by most people, but an autumn sowing has the advantage of exposing the seeds to cold frosty weather. Several types of wildflower, particularly the pea family, cranesbills and primulas (Cowslips and Primroses), will show better germination after freezing weather, as will the important species Yellow Rattle.

Meadow seed ready for sowing

Your next step is to calculate the amount of seed you will need. **A sowing rate of 4 g for each square meter of ground is recommended,** but even a little less will give good results. Most good specialist wildflower seed growers will give advice over the telephone if you are having difficulty working out what you need. If you are sowing a large area you may want to bulk up the seed with something like silver sand – this shows up on the soil surface and makes it easier to sow evenly. For larger areas an old-fashioned seed fiddle can be used, or where the area is accessible to machinery a seed drill will give good results. Make sure that the seed is well mixed before you start, as some species have very small seeds and these will drop to the bottom of your container.

If you are sowing by hand, simply walk up and down the area concerned scattering the seed as you go. **You can**

Rolling after sowing

divide up the space into sections with coloured string, if this will aid even distribution. When all the seed has gone, walk methodically over the area pushing the seeds into the soil with your feet. A garden roller is also effective for this. The idea is to ensure that you have good seed to soil contact, but the seed must not be covered with soil, so don't be tempted to rake it in. Some wildflowers germinate better when they are exposed to light – covering them with soil will hinder germination.

All that remains is to protect the area from seed-eating birds and to water lightly if no rain is forthcoming. For bird protection a few shiny old CDs or DVDs hanging around the area seem to work very well, or **coloured string around the perimeter will help prevent larger birds such as Pheasants and Wood Pigeons walking into the area**. This is a particular problem in my rural garden, but the pheasants are definitely deterred by this approach. Avoid netting the area though, as birds can become entangled. By and large a few birds won't make a huge amount of difference to your area, especially if you have pressed the seed into the soil well.

As soon as your meadow area starts to germinate, you will need to think about the work now involved in getting it well established and maintaining its diversity of species. You will find that information in Chapter 7.

First year

Second year

Quaking Grass

CHAPTER THREE

Customising your Wildflower Meadow

Meadows are very dynamic habitats, and the species composition can, and will, change naturally from year to year. In a garden situation we may, to a certain extent, manipulate the diversity of an area by adding plants that we particularly like or think will especially benefit wildlife, as long as those plants are suited to the conditions.

Corn Poppy

Adding cornfield flowers

One way of giving your new meadow a real boost of colour in its first year is to combine a meadow seed mix for your soil type with seeds of the cornfield annuals already mentioned, including Corn Poppy, Cornflower, Corn Marigold and Corncockle. The true meadow wildflowers may take some time to get established (with the exception of Oxeye Daisies, which generally do well in their first year), so some bright flowers in the first summer will be very welcome. It is important to remember that these annuals will not persist much beyond the first summer – they need disturbed soil in which to germinate and flourish. If you really enjoy their bright colours and their ability to attract a wide range of insects, sow them in a special bed of their own in future years. You can find information about this in Chapter 6.

If you wish to modify your first-year meadow in this way, **for every 10 g**

Corn Marigold with Soldier Beetle

Corncockle

Dropwort

Common Spotted Orchid

of meadow mix you use add 5 g of cornfield annual seeds. Make sure you combine the mixtures well, as the poppy seeds are very small and will fall to the bottom of the mix. This mixture can be sown in autumn or spring.

Adding your favourite species

If there are particular meadow flowers that you would like to see in your garden, and they are not included in the mixture you buy, you can add seed as long as they are perennial flowers, suitable for your soil, and true meadow plants that can grow amongst grasses. In my previous garden, where the sandy soil was very dry and free draining, I added the seed of Dropwort, a dry grassland species, to a meadow mix. Its creamy flowers are a particular favourite of mine, and they enhanced the meadow admirably. My current garden is on heavy clay, and my new meadow had several extra species added that thrive in this type of soil. Just 0.1 g of the seeds of Common Spotted Orchid were added to the mix at sowing time. The result has been over 200 orchids appearing within six years of sowing – a very exciting result!

Add just a few grams of seed of your chosen plant – if it enjoys the conditions in your soil it will spread of its own accord, or you can collect seed from the seed heads later in the year if you wish and grow more small plants as plugs plants (see Appendix) to add later. Alternatively if the species is happy, it should spread slowly of its own accord.

Sowing Yellow Rattle

Yellow Rattle is rather a special plant. Some meadow mixes will already contain the seed of this annual – one of the few such plants that can successfully be established in a perennial wildflower meadow. It is unusual in that it is partially parasitic on the roots of certain native grasses and has the effect of reducing their vigour. Establishing this plant will help to prevent grasses in a new meadow from swamping the flowers, and in my experience it can reduce the height of the grass by as much as a third, making it easier to cut in the autumn and giving the wildflowers space to grow and making their flowers more prominent.

Yellow Rattle is best sown in September or October as it needs a good hard winter to stimulate the seed to germinate in the following spring. It will not germinate in bare soil – it needs the grasses and will not grow without them, so it can be sown onto an already established meadow area or included in your mix for an autumn

Yellow Rattle

Yellow Rattle seed

Yellow Rattle seedpods

Yellow Rattle in flower

sowing. Yellow Rattle gets its name from the rattling of the large ripe seeds inside the seedpod. The rattling was used in the past to indicate that the hay crop was ready to cut in late June and July – in garden meadows we tend to cut later in the year in order to get maximum enjoyment from the flowers all through the summer months, plus provide greater benefit to the meadow wildlife.

Adding plug plants to your established meadow

One other way of enhancing a garden meadow is to add plug plants (see page 61) in future years. You may want to include new species that you particularly like, or some that are especially good for wildlife. You can even add extra grasses, such as Quaking Grass, which is easy to grow from seed. With the exception of Yellow Rattle, it is difficult to get wildflowers to establish from seed scattered onto an existing meadow, but plug plants added in autumn or spring when the meadow is short are generally very successful. Once established, these will continue to spread as long as they are happy and suited to your soil type and the maintenance you employ. You can get these from a specialist grower or try growing your own using the information in the Appendix.

Quaking Grass

Sometimes, either through perfectly natural changes or through poor management of your meadow, plant species will disappear over time. These can also be reintroduced as plugs if you wish, although it is worth remembering that they might have disappeared as a result of the conditions not being quite right for them. All meadows change over time, and this succession is a perfectly natural ecological occurrence.

Existing lawn with White Clover

CHAPTER FOUR

Creating a Meadow Effect in Existing Grass

Sometimes there may be areas in gardens where the removal of existing grass could be a major undertaking. These areas may include well-spaced orchard trees or large, unused lawns that could be put to better use and attract more wildlife. Areas like this can also take up our time, particularly with mowing. So is it possible to convert an area of grass to meadow, and if so, how do we go about it?

What sort of grass do you have?

It is possible to create a meadow effect in an existing grass area, but it is by no means as simple as starting from scratch. This should always be the preferred option where there is a choice. When starting with existing grass, there is one important consideration at the outset – what

sort of grass already grows in the area? **Existing grass should be fine leaved and evenly distributed.** As we have seen from the seed mixes available, the grasses included in them are fine-leaved, non-invasive native species such as the fescues (*Festuca* species), amongst which wildflowers will thrive and spread. Grasses that grow more aggressively, such as Cocksfoot, Couch or Rye Grass are too tough and competitive to produce a diverse meadow area with lots of different wildflowers. In fact in areas such as these, only the toughest wildflowers will survive – others will simply disappear after a year or two. There are species of wildflower that will survive in rough grass, and these are mentioned in Chapter 5, but in general you need to ensure that the grasses already established in the area are suitable for a meadow.

Clover in fine grasses

Tough grasses

Few of us can identify species of wild grasses, but there are two good rough indicators of grass type for complete beginners:

- Are the grass leaves broad and tough, or narrow and needle-like?
- Do they grow in big clumps?

If the majority of the grass is narrow leaved and distributed evenly throughout the lawn, it should be possible to add wildflowers for a meadow effect. If the grasses are growing in dense clumps and get very tall if left uncut, or if the leaves are dark green and very shiny (an indication of rye grass) it could be a difficult task to add flowers, with a few exceptions (see Chapter 5). Another indicator could be the age of your house. Older properties may well have lawns made of the fine-leaved fescue grasses, whereas newer housing is more likely to have a rye grass lawn. One thing is certain; no amount of seed spread onto anything other than the most sparsely covered, neglected lawn will produce a meadow. Seed, money and time will be wasted, so do not be tempted to try this.

Your options

If you have determined that the majority of your grasses are narrow leaved, slow growing and well behaved, there are three options open to you:

Uncut area of lawn grass with buttercups

- You can attempt to distribute a meadow mix for your soil type after preparation of the area, as long as the lawn is sparse and thin.
- You can add summer flowering wildflower plugs suitable for your soil type.
- You can add early flowering wildflower plugs and bulbs to produce a spring meadow.

Adding seed to sparse lawns

By and large scattering seed onto grass does not produce a meadow, so this option will only work on very poor, patchy and badly maintained areas of grass or moss, plus some hard work will be necessary. As with all seed sowing, **the seed must make direct contact with the soil**, so for this option to produce good results bare soil must be exposed. In garden areas, this can be done by cutting the grass as short as possible and then raking hard to expose areas of bare soil. A meadow mixture of seeds suitable for your soil can then be distributed onto the surface and pressed in with the feet, concentrating on the barest patches. Watering and bird protection should then be carried out in the same way as for a meadow sown onto bare soil. On larger areas of land, where access with machinery is not a problem, a chain harrow can be used to expose bare soil. This option is best carried out in the autumn to allow the seeds a little space to germinate. In the spring months they may be swamped by growth of the existing grasses.

Adding wildflower plugs

Wildflower plants can be added to existing fine grass areas and will be most successful if introduced as plug plants. These are small plants in their own little plug of soil and can be bought from various nurseries around the country (see Appendix on page 63 for suppliers). Plant them by removing a small divot of short grass or bare soil and firm them into the hole. Water frequently unless the weather is very wet. Plug plants can be added in spring or autumn and should be placed as randomly as possible for a natural effect. To grow your own plugs, see the instructions in the Appendix (page 61).

Making a spring-flowering meadow

A spring-flowering meadow is a good option for a garden where there are many users – it can look colourful and attract insects and small mammals, and birds in the spring and early summer, but can revert to general usage at the end of June once it has been cut and raked off, in time for the school holidays! After the initial cut, a spring meadow may be mown along with other lawns with no detriment to the wildflowers. Another advantage of establishing a spring meadow is that many of the bulbs and plants mentioned below, which are suitable for this treatment, will tolerate some shade.

You could include bulbs such as Wild Daffodil, Star of Bethlehem or Snake's

Star of Bethlehem

Snake's Head Fritillary

Cowslip

Ragged Robin

Head Fritillary (depending on your soil type), and Cowslips are a perfect choice, being adaptable to wet or dry soils and freely spreading if the seed is allowed to drop before the area is cut. Ragged Robin and Lady's Smock are other early flowerers which will have set seed by the end of June. Add your wildflower plugs and bulbs as described above during September or October. For other species suitable for a spring meadow, in wet or dry soils, turn to the table on page 62.

Maintenance of your meadow, whether it has been produced from seeds or plug plants, is described in Chapter 7.

Lady's Smock

Red Clover and native grasses

CHAPTER FIVE
Meadow Flowers in Rough Grass

Many of us have areas in our gardens where there might be rough grass, brambles, nettles and all manner of 'weeds' that we would prefer not to have to deal with. Larger gardens may have neglected orchards or old lawns that have been invaded by weedy plants. The idea of converting an area such as this to a wildflower meadow buzzing with butterflies, bees and birds is very appealing, but this is not necessarily an easy task.

A proper meadow in such an area could only be made by starting with bare soil and following the instructions in Chapter 2. However, there are plants that will cope with tougher grasses and even thrive amongst them.

Converting a rough grass area to grasses with wildflowers

Before adding wildflowers to a rough grass area a certain amount of work will need to be carried out. **But before you start, take a close look to see whether a variety of wildlife is already using the area.** Will you be disturbing Hedgehogs and other mammals? Are there brambles providing food for voles, mice and birds or nectar for bees and butterflies? Brambles are also wonderful nesting places for small birds such as warblers. Nettle is the larval food plant of several of our prettiest butterflies, and tall grasses provide shelter for many invertebrates, including several species

Bank Vole

Greenfinch (above) and House Sparrow, seed eaters

Hogweed

Cow Parsley

Meadow Buttercup

But if you are sure that your plans will definitely enhance the wildlife value of the area, begin by removing the brambles or other shrubby vegetation. A heavy duty mower, used regularly over the area during the growing season, will help to get rid of plants like nettles and the tougher grasses, but check nettles thoroughly for caterpillars and leave any plants being used until the larvae have pupated. In fact, regular mowing of a rough area like this will help to eliminate Hogweed, Cow Parsley, nettles, docks, brambles and several other plants that may swamp your new wildflowers, without you having to resort to the use of chemicals.

Plan well in advance. By mowing and removing the cuttings every couple of weeks through spring and summer, your area should be in a better condition to allow the establishment of wildflower plugs in the autumn or following spring.

The table on page 62 provides a list of wildflowers that are tough enough to cope with less than ideal meadow conditions.

These plants can be added as plugs, obtainable from specialist wildflower nurseries, or you could try growing your own from seed using the basic instructions in the Appendix. **Always chose native seed and plugs from a reputable supplier** who guarantees that the plants are of native origin (see page 63).

of butterfly and lots of native moths. First give some thought as to whether changing the area is going to be to the detriment of the creatures already living there. It may be that the best thing, from the point of view of your existing garden wildlife, is to leave the area exactly as it is in an undisturbed state.

Don't forget that once wildflowers are growing in your grassy area you will need to cut and rake it every autumn, as outlined in Chapter 7, to keep it looking really good, to encourage the flowers to spread and to ensure it is a good habitat for a variety of wildlife.

Clockwise from top left:

Wild Marjoram, Yarrow, Red Clover, Common Knapweed, Field Scabious, Tufted Vetch

47

Cornfield annuals

CHAPTER SIX

Growing Cornfield Flowers

Many gardeners love the idea of growing colourful annual wildflowers. As we have already seen in this guide, an area of these flowers is not strictly a meadow as it contains no native grasses but is nonetheless a wonderful wildlife habitat and especially attractive to insects. If you particularly like these flowers you can make a bed especially for them. **This is an easy and straightforward task** and creates an area of colourful wildflowers which will bloom all through the summer, attract a huge range of insects and some seed-eating birds, and provide interest in the autumn with pretty seed heads.

Many of the annual flowers that once grew along the edges, and sometimes in the midst, of our wheat, oat and barley fields have been eradicated over time. Poppies and Cornflowers occasionally pop up on agricultural land after ploughing or even alongside roads where the verges have been disturbed, but mostly now they are unusual species in our countryside. However, seed mixes of these now scarce flowers can be purchased from a variety of seed merchants and catalogues. To ensure your local wildlife is attracted to the plants, choose a supplier from page 63 in order to obtain plant species that are of native origin.

These mixtures usually consist of five annual species:

Corn Poppy, also known as Field Poppy, is a familiar plant to us all, with its tissue paper thin, scarlet petals and black centre. It flowers in June

Corn Poppies

Corn Marigold

Cornflower

Corncockle

and July, and sporadically throughout the rest of the summer. It produces copious amounts of pollen and is therefore a good source of food for honeybees, bumblebees, solitary bees and hoverflies.

Corn Marigold is much less common now than it once was. This is a bright yellow daisy that attracts a wide variety of insects, especially honeybees, bumblebees and the smaller species of butterfly, including the Common Blue, Small Copper and the skippers.

Cornflower is a plant most of us know, even though we might never have seen it in the wild, and the intense blue of the petals is a wonderfully pure colour. Growing these delicate flowers is a very good way of encouraging smaller butterflies such as the Common Blue to the garden, and in the autumn acrobatic Goldfinches will come to tease the large seeds from the seed heads.

Corncockle has round black seeds which follow the attractive dark pink flowers. These seeds are poisonous, so it was eradicated from cornfields in the recent past. It is probably not a native wildflower but an ancient introduction from the Mediterranean that naturalised over many years and became common in our fields, only to disappear again. It will attract all sorts of bees and hoverflies. On account of its poisonous nature you may wish to choose a mixture without it.

Corn Chamomile with Gatekeeper

Corn Chamomile

Corn Chamomile has masses of small white daisy flowers and is vital to the whole mix. Its white flowers provide a background to the other bright colours, while attracting a huge range of smaller insects, especially hoverflies.

As well as these five species, some cornfield flower mixes contain other annual species, including Scarlet Pimpernel, Night-flowering Catchfly, White Campion, Mayweed and Field Forget-me-not. These all add their own character to the overall effect. You can also add a handful of Barley or Wheat seed if you wish, for a really 'rural' feel.

An area of these native annuals in your garden will enhance its wildlife value, as well as looking spectacular in

White Campion

Calendula

Nigella

even quite a small space. Many other annual mixtures are available, but these often include non-native plants such as *Calendula*, Love-in-a-mist or *Nigella*, Borage or Larkspur. These widely available mixtures can be valuable as insect attractants but will not create the same natural effect as our own native cornfield annuals.

Growing your cornfield flowers

If you are inspired to sow a cornfield area in your garden, you should first decide where to locate it. Because these wildflowers are all annual species, individually they do not take up a huge amount of space, so this mixture can be grown in a large container or trough in smaller gardens. If this appeals to you, it would be necessary to use a very poor quality soil in your container to make sure the plants did not get too big – potting compost in this situation could produce too much soft growth

Holly Blue on Borage

and too few flowers, plus the plants will flop and sprawl. If you are making a wildlife pond, the subsoil from the bottom of the hole is ideal for these species.

Small areas of these lovely flowers can brighten a sunny corner or fill spaces between shrubs in a newly planted border, but the colours are so dramatic I always sow the biggest area I can accommodate.

Choosing your site

Dedicating a small bed specifically to these cornfield flowers creates a pretty effect with great impact, and if you can't find space between existing plants you may want to consider a patch in a vegetable area if you have one. The beneficial insects these plants attract will make up for the loss of space for vegetables. However, this is definitely a project when 'big is best', and the impact these flowers make means that, if you have space, sow a

Large cornfield bed

large patch. What is important is that, as with 'proper' meadow creation, the area must be as free as possible of perennial weeds. Use the same methods to remove weeds as for a wildflower meadow – digging them out may be the hardest option in terms of work, but it is generally the most effective in the long run.

When to sow…

Cornfield flower areas, like true meadows, can be sown in spring or autumn. In springtime, the months of March and April are best, or an autumn sowing in September or October will also work well. There are advantages and disadvantages to both times. Like our native cowslips, vetches and trefoils, Corn Poppies germinate best when the seeds have been exposed to cold, frosty weather – thus sowing in the spring may mean that these seeds will not germinate to their full potential if the frosts have passed. They will, of course, germinate in the next spring, as poppy seeds can remain viable for up to 100 years. On the other hand, an autumn sowing may mean that some seed will be

Cornfield area

eaten by birds, voles and Wood Mice through the winter months, and it is possible that autumn germinators such as Corncockle may dominate the effect in the following summer. Whichever you opt for, these are all species that germinate easily.

…and how

Once the soil is free of weeds and has been raked down to a reasonable tilth, you can begin the sowing. This operation is similar to sowing a meadow, only this time the sowing rate is less – **only 2 g per square metre will produce well-covered soil and plenty of bright flowers**. Again, if the area is large, try adding silver sand to the seeds to aid an even distribution. Sow the seed by scattering it as evenly as possible, or for larger areas a seed drill or seed fiddle could be used. It is not a crucial operation – an uneven distribution will correct itself in coming years as the plants self-sow in the autumn to flower the next year. Generally the plants themselves make a better job of it than we do.

Once all the seed is scattered, walk up and down as with a meadow mixture, pressing it into the soil with your feet making sure that you don't cover the seeds with soil. Poppies in particular need light to germinate, so the last thing you want to do is cover them up by raking soil over them. Water lightly if the weather is very dry, but you should see seedlings within a couple of weeks. A shiny old CD or DVD will

again give the seeds a fighting chance if you have lots of finches or House Sparrows around. All that is necessary after that is to sit back and admire!

To keep your cornfield patch going, you will need to do some maintenance in the autumn. This is covered in Chapter 7.

Meadow area after cutting with a scythe

CHAPTER 7
Wildflower Meadow and Cornfield Flower Maintenance

Once you have established your meadow or cornfield area, it is vital that you carry out maintenance work every autumn to allow it to flourish. A meadow left to its own devices will soon lose its species diversity. Some of the tougher wildflowers may survive, but in general many of the flowering species will suffer and even slowly die out if the meadow is not cut and the hay removed from it on an annual basis. It is essential that you have this commitment to your meadow before you begin, or you will be disappointed with the results in the long term.

Maintenance of your wildflower meadow in Year 1

Almost as soon as your meadow seed starts to germinate, a decision must be made. In order to encourage the flowers to establish, it is generally recommended that the newly growing plants are cut all through the first spring and summer to a height of between 5 and 10 cm (2 and 4 inches), *unless* you have added cornfield flowers. Cutting in this way will keep the grasses under control, while the wildflowers get established. This is very hard to do – the temptation to see the beginnings of your new habitat is very strong! If you decide you cannot cut in the first spring and summer, or you have added cornfield annuals that must be allowed to grow up and flower, do not worry unduly. The meadow will survive, but

a few species may take a little longer to get going. I have never been able to bring myself to cut a meadow in its first year – it is far too exciting to watch it develop.

Cutting the meadow in August or September, once most of the wildflowers have finished flowering, is crucial, however small the area, and in general a lawn mower is not suitable for this job. Mowers chop the grass too much, producing a mulch of grass fragments on the soil surface which we want to avoid. Cutting with an old-fashioned hand scythe is very efficient, but it is hard work and takes a degree of skill. A strimmer can be used but is not ideal. For larger areas a motorised scythe (or Allen scythe) is a good option, and these can be rented from tool hire firms. However you decide to cut, choose a warm dry day if possible, as the whole process is easier if the grass is not soaking wet. Take your time and look out for small mammals and amphibians as you go. Small areas can be cut very efficiently with hand shears, but for really large meadows it may be necessary to contact a local farmer and have the area professionally cut and baled.

Cut to a height of between 5 to 10 cm (2 to 4 inches) and leave the hay for a few days to dry. During this time the seeds will fall to the ground, ready to replenish the flowers and grasses, allowing then to spread. Your next job is to rake all the cuttings off. Each year as you rake off the hay the fertility of the soil is reduced, which benefits the wildflowers. Most importantly, raking opens up the turf, exposing small areas of bare soil where the wildflower seeds that have fallen can germinate. The raking should be vigorous – don't be surprised if the area looks patchy as a result – this is what you want. For larger areas the alternative here is to use a chain harrow or even borrow a sheep or two to crop the grass.

You may want to cut the area a few more times in the autumn – the mower will suffice here as long as you **set the blade on the highest cut and remove the clippings.**

Subsequent years – a summer-flowering meadow...

The strategy above, used in subsequent years, will keep your meadow established and encourage the wildflowers to spread. If your meadow has mainly summer flowers (no Cowslips for instance) you can also now cut a couple of times in March and April if you wish, again with the mower blade on a high cut and the clippings removed.

...and a spring-flowering meadow

Even if your meadow contains Cowslips, spring bulbs, Bugle, Lady's Smock or any other spring-flowering plants, the

Cutting with a scythe

maintenance is exactly the same – only the timing is different. All the activities occur earlier in the year, so there is no cutting in spring; the main cut and rake is in July, and subsequent cuts must be high and the clippings removed.

If you have a meadow with spring *and* summer flowers (a combination meadow), follow the guidelines for the summer meadow and avoid all cutting until August/September.

Annual maintenance of a cornfield area

Cornfield flowers are all annuals and as such produce plenty of seeds for replenishing themselves year after year. Once these areas are sown they can be left entirely to their own devices until September, when all the dead flower stalks can be pulled out. Make sure that you shake out all available seeds at this time – they will fall back to the soil to germinate for the coming year.

It may be necessary to **dig out any perennial weedy species that have found their way into your cornfield flowers** at this point. Docks, thistles, nettles and other weedy species will invade the area, given half a chance. Gently fork these plants out without creating too much disturbance. Once you are happy with the area, walk up and down on it to push the seeds back into the soil with your feet.

Occasionally the balance of species shifts in a cornfield area. Corncockles

Cuttings drying in haystacks

are autumn germinators and can sometimes dominate in subsequent years. If this is the case, simple turn over with a spade a few patches in October or March and bury them. You will turn up the seeds of other species to germinate in their place. In small areas, you can weed a few Corncockles out by hand if they become dominant.

If you find that one species is disappearing altogether, add a little seed of this to the area in the early spring.

Neat path edging

Summary of meadow and cornfield maintenance

All cutting should be to a height of 5 to 10cm (2 to 4 inches).

Spring Meadows
- Allow to grow up and flower from March to July.
- Scythe and rake off the hay in July.
- Continue to cut occasionally between July and October using a mower on the highest cut with the grass box in place.

Summer Meadows
- Cut occasionally in March and April if you wish using a mower on the highest cut with the grass box in place.
- Allow to grow up and flower from April to August/September.
- Scythe and rake off hay in August or September.

- Continue to cut occasionally in autumn if you wish using a mower on the highest cut with the grass box in place.

Combination Meadows – where a summer meadow also contains Cowslips or other early flowers.
- Allow to grow up and flower between March and August/September.
- Scythe and rake off hay in August or September.
- Continue to cut occasionally in autumn if you wish using a mower on the highest cut with the grass box in place.

Rough Grass with Wildflowers
- Follow directions for Combination meadows.

Growing wildflower plugs from seed

Growing your own wildflower plants from seed requires a little knowledge and a lot of patience. Many species can be grown from seed in trays or pots and then grown on as plug plants to add to a meadow at a later date. The best time to sow wildflower seed, if you are a beginner, is the autumn. Many wildflowers need a long period of cold and frost before they will germinate, so let the natural elements outside provide the conditions that these seeds require.

Bladder Campion, added as a plug plant

Fill your pot or seed tray with a soil-based John Innes type compost. Don't be tempted to sow huge quantities of seed – a small amount of the easier to germinate wildflowers, such as Oxeye Daisy or Knapweed will probably produce more seedlings than you can handle. Scatter the seed as evenly as possible on the soil surface and then cover with a very thin layer of horticultural grit or vermiculite. This will deter fungal diseases such as 'damping off', which can cause rapid seedling death. If the seeds are exceptionally small, sow them *on top* of the grit. Tiny seeds will fail to germinate if they are buried too deeply. Make sure that you label the pots with a weather-proof marker pen.

Once the seed is sown, leave the pots outside in a place where they will benefit from the winter weather conditions. Make sure that they don't dry out at any time. Germination will happen in early spring, but don't expect all the seeds to germinate at the same time. Some species may continue to germinate from a seed tray over the next year or more. As the seedlings appear and are large enough to handle, (this will vary considerably with species), you can prick them out into plugs filled with the same soil-based compost and grow them on in a sheltered place.

Most wildflowers sown in autumn will produce seedlings in March. If they are pricked out at this time, the plug plants will usually be large enough to plant out into your meadow in late spring. If they are not, keep them growing on in their plugs until the autumn and transplant them when the meadow has been cut and raked.

Once you have a bit more experience and you know the different conditions that your wildflower seeds require in order to germinate, you will be able to sow species in spring and autumn and add new species to your meadow over time.

Some wildflowers suitable for growing in meadow grass

D – dry or well-draining soil   **W** – wet or clay soil   **T** – tough grasses

Plant species	Latin name	Conditions		
		D	W	T
Betony	Stachys officinalis	●	●	
Birdsfoot Trefoil	Lotus corniculatus	●	●	
Bladder Campion	Silene vulgaris	●		
Common Knapweed	Centaurea nigra	●	●	●
Common Sorrel	Rumex acetosa	●	●	●
Cowslip	Primula veris	●	●	●
Devil's-bit Scabious	Succisa pratensis		●	
Dropwort	Filipendula vulgaris	●		
Field Scabious	Knautia arvensis	●		●
Greater Knapweed	Centaurea scabiosa	●		●
Hoary Plantain	Plantago media	●		
Lady's Bedstraw	Galium verum	●	●	
Meadow Buttercup	Ranunculus acris		●	●
Meadow Cranesbill	Geranium pratense	●	●	●
Meadowsweet	Filipendula ulmaria		●	
Musk Mallow	Malva moschata	●		
Oxeye Daisy	Leucanthemum vulgare	●	●	●
Quaking Grass	Briza media	●		
Ragged Robin	Lychnis flos-cuculi		●	
Red Clover	Trifolium pratense	●	●	●
Salad Burnet	Sanguisorba minor	●	●	●
Selfheal	Prunella vulgaris	●	●	
Sheep's Sorrel	Rumex acetosella	●		
Snake's Head Fritillary	Fritillaria meleagris		●	
Sneezewort	Achillea ptarmica		●	
Tufted Vetch	Vicia cracca	●	●	●
Wild Basil	Clinopodium vulgare	●		
Wild Carrot	Daucus carota	●		
Wild Marjoram	Origanum vulgare	●		●
Yarrow	Achillea millefolium	●		●
Yellow Rattle	Rhinanthus minor	●	●	●

Further Information

Suppliers of Native Seeds and Plants

Emorsgate Seeds: Limes Farm,
Tilney All Saints, Kings Lynn,
Norfolk PE34 4RT,
Tel: 01553 829028,
www.wildseed.co.uk

Habitataid: Hookgate Cottage,
South Brewham, Somerset BA10 0LQ,
Tel: 01749 812355,
www.habitataid.co.uk

Chiltern Seeds Ltd:
Crowmarsh Battle Barns,
114 Preston Crowmarsh,
Wallingford, OX10 6SL,
Tel. 01491 824675,
www.chilternseeds.co.uk

Jenny Steel's website
www.wildlife-gardening.co.uk has a
complete guide to wildlife gardening,
including updated lists of suppliers.

Further Reading

Lewis, Pam (2003) *Making Wildflower Meadows*. Frances Lincoln, London, 160pp.

Lloyd, Christopher & Buckley, Jonathan (2004) *Meadows*. Timber Press, Portland, Oregon, USA, 192pp.

Thomas, Adrian (2010) *Gardening for Wildlife – a Complete Guide to Nature-Friendly Gardening*. A & C Black, London, 240pp.

Wilson, Matthew (2011) *Nature's Gardener – How to Garden in the 21st Century*. Mitchell Beazley, London, 224pp.

Other Publications by Jenny Steel

Wildflower Gardening – wildflowers for every garden situation. Webbs Barn Designs, Kingston Bagpuize, Oxon (2007) 98pp.

Bringing a Garden to Life. Wiggly Wigglers, Blakemere, Herefordshire (2006) 160pp.

Butterfly Gardening – How to encourage butterflies to your garden. Webbs Barn Designs, Kingston Bagpuize, Oxon (2003) 32pp.

Wildlife Ponds – how to create a natural looking pond to attract wildlife to your garden. Webbs Barn Designs, Kingston Bagpuize, Oxon (2002) 32pp.

Wildflowers for Wildlife – plants to make your garden wildlife friendly. Osmia Publications, Loughborough, Leicestershire (2001) 46pp.

Wildlife Organisations

Butterfly Conservation:
Manor Yard, East Lulworth, Wareham, Dorset BH20 5QP,
Tel. 01929 400209,
www.butterfly-conservation.org

The Wildlife Trusts:
The Kiln, Waterside, Mather Road, Newark, Nottinghamshire NG24 1WT,
Tel. 01636 677711,
www.wildlifetrusts.org

Flora Locale:
provide lists of British and Irish Flora suppliers.
Postern Hill Lodge, Marlborough, Wiltshire, SN8 4ND,
Tel. 01672 515723,
www.floralocale.org

Other nature books by Brambleby Books

British and Irish Butterflies –
The complete Field, Identification
and Site Guide to the Species, Subspecies
and Forms
by Adrian M. Riley
ISBN 9780955392801

The Flora of Berkshire
by Michael J. Crawley
ISBN 9780954334741

The Wild Flowers of the Isles of Purbeck,
Brownsea and Sandbank
by Edward Pratt
ISBN 9780955392849

Garden Photo Shoot – A Photographer's
Year-book of Garden Wildlife
by John Thurlbourn
ISBN 9780955392832

Never a dull moment – A naturalist's view
of British wildlife
by Ross Gardner
ISBN 9780955392870

Norfolk Wildlife –
A Calendar and Site Guide
by Adrian M. Riley
ISBN 9781908241047

www.bramblebybooks.co.uk

Notes

Brambleby Books